THE END OF THE TOUR

Joel Drake Johnson

I0140076

BROADWAY PLAY PUBLISHING INC
New York
www.broadwayplaypublishing.com
info@broadwayplaypublishing.com

THE END OF THE TOUR
© Copyright 2007 by Joel Drake Johnson

First printing: February 2007
I S B N: 0-88145-332-3

Book design: Marie Donovan
Word processing: Microsoft Word
Typographic controls: Ventura Publisher
Typeface: Palatino

CHARACTERS & SETTING

JAN (MORRIS) WILLIAMSON, *forty-eight to fifty*
ANDREW MORRIS, *thirty-seven to forty, her younger brother*
MAE (MORRIS) PIERCE, *sixty-eight to seventy, her mother*
CHUCK WILLIAMSON, *fifity to fifty-one*, JAN*'s husband*
DAVID SABIN, *thirty-five to thirty-eight*, ANDREW*'s
    boyfriend*
TOMMY JOHNS, *forty-eight to fifty, a friend of* CHUCK*'s*
NORMA, *ancient, a patient*

Place: various locations of Dixon, Illinois

THE END OF THE TOUR received its world premiere at Victory Gardens Theater (Artistic director, Dennis Zacek; Managing Director, Marcie McVay) in Chicago, Illinois, on 23 May 2003. The cast and creative contributors were as follows:

JAN	Annabel Armour
ANDREW	Timothy Hendrickson
CHUCK	Rob Riley
DAVID	Andrew Rothenberg
TOMMY	Marc Silvia
MAE	Mary Ann Thebus
NORMA	Kitty Tabor
Director	Sandy Shinner
Set design	Jeff Bauer
Lighting design	Rita Pietraszek
Sound design	Andre Pluess
Costume design	Judith Lundberg

for Sandy Shinner and Marc Silvia

thanks to Larry B Salzmann, Jeff Storer,
and Lynn Baber

(A spot comes up on JAN *who is standing by a phone. Beat.* JAN *picks up the phone and dials. She hangs up. Beat.* JAN *dials again. She hangs up. She paces and then picks up the phone to dial. A phone rings in another spot.* ANDREW *stumbles to answer it.)*

ANDREW: *(As the lights come up)* Hello.

JAN: Andrew? It's Jan.

ANDREW: Who?

DAVID: Who is it?

ANDREW: I don't know.

JAN: It's Jan. Your sister

ANDREW: Did Mom die?

JAN: No.

DAVID: *(Overlapping)* What time is it?

JAN: Did you get my messages? I left you—

ANDREW: I got your messages. I got all your messages.

DAVID: Who is it?

ANDREW: My sister.

JAN: I'm sorry to call so late. I couldn't sleep.
I was pacing—

ANDREW: You woke me up.

JAN: Are you coming?

DAVID: *(Overlapping)* Why is she calling so late?
Is your mom dead?

ANDREW: *(Overlapping)* We hadn't planned on coming, no. *(To* DAVID*)* She wants to know if we're coming.

JAN: Who are you talking to?

DAVID: *(Overlapping)* Did your mom die?

ANDREW: David.

JAN: What?

ANDREW: It's David. His name is David.

JAN: Another boyfriend?

ANDREW: I beg your pardon—

JAN: I'm sorry. I wasn't—

ANDREW: If this isn't an emergency—even if it is an emergency—

JAN: Mom's depressed. She's in a nursing home—

ANDREW: I know all this—

JAN: Then why haven't you—it's been close to a month—

ANDREW: Do you know what time it is? This is really upsetting me.

DAVID: *(Into phone)* Don't upset my boyfriend.

ANDREW: I'm not coming home. I'd have to take a day off work—it's not—

JAN: I've taken days off—

ANDREW: And I can't drive—

JAN: You can drive—

ANDREW: I lost my driver's license—

JAN: How did you—

ANDREW: I flunked the test and I refuse to go back—

JAN: You should have a driver's license—

ANDREW: No, I shouldn't—fuck this—

JAN: What did I do to you? What did I ever do to you?

ANDREW: It's after midnight—

JAN: I would like to know. I was always supportive of you. I was always protective—

ANDREW: *(He hands phone to* DAVID*)* I can't talk to her. You talk to her.

JAN: *(Overlapping)* What did I ever do?

DAVID: *(Overlapping)* I don't know her. I've never met her—

JAN: *(Overlapping)* Hello? Andy? Andrew?

DAVID: Hello. He's upset. You've upset him.

JAN: Can you get him back on the phone?

DAVID: I don't want you to upset him. He'll never get to sleep now. Never. You shouldn't have done this—

JAN: I just want him to come home—

ANDREW: *(Overlapping)* Hang up, okay? Just hang up.

DAVID: *(Overlapping)* He doesn't want to come home— *(To* ANDREW*)* You come over here and hang up.

JAN: Do I sound like I want to hurt him? What has he said—

ANDREW: *(Overlapping)* What is she saying?

DAVID: *(To* ANDREW*)* Shhhh.

ANDREW: Don't shush me!

DAVID: *(To* ANDREW*)* Will you come back to the phone?

ANDREW: No, I will not come back to the phone—

DAVID: He won't come back—

JAN: I heard him.

DAVID: Sorry.

ANDREW: Don't apologize for me.

DAVID: I'm not.

JAN: He really needs to deal with this.

ANDREW: What's she saying?

DAVID: Well...

JAN: I'm sorry. Maybe you can convince him.

DAVID: He's a hard sell—

ANDREW: What is she saying?

JAN: But maybe you could. He shouldn't let this go like that. David? Is that your name? David?

DAVID: David, yes. Nice to meet you.

JAN: Do you love him, David?

ANDREW: What is—

DAVID: *(To* ANDREW*)* Shhh. *(To* JAN*)* Yes. Yes, I do.

JAN: Me, too. I love him, too.

DAVID: Oh... Hold on a second. *(To* ANDREW*)* I think we should go.

*(*ANDREW *drops his head. Beat)*

DAVID: Andrew?

ANDREW: What?!

*(*DAVID *holds phone out to* ANDREW*. Beat.)*

DAVID: Take the phone.

ANDREW: *(Overlapping)* Don't tell me what to do. Don't tell me what to do.

DAVID: *(Overlapping)* Take the phone. Take the phone.

*(*ANDREW *comes to the phone.)*

ANDREW: Jan.

JAN: Yes?

ANDREW: It's Andrew.

JAN: I—

ANDREW: *(Quickly)* And okay. We'll come. Tomorrow. *(To* DAVID*)* Tomorrow's okay?

DAVID: Tomorrow's fine.

ANDREW: *(To* JAN*)* Tomorrow?

JAN: Okay.

ANDREW: Alright.

JAN: She's in the Lee County Nursing Home.

ANDREW: You'll be there?

JAN: I'll be there.

ANDREW: Chuck?

JAN: No, no Chuck.

ANDREW: Okay, then. Sometime tomorrow...ummm, it's good to hear from you—

JAN: It is?

ANDREW: Good night.

JAN: Good night.

(She hangs up. As she pauses at phone, ANDREW *and* DAVID *stare at one another.)*

ANDREW: This is not something I want to do. I want to forget this shit—

DAVID: I'll be with you, Andrew.

(Pause)

ANDREW: I'll have to make a couple of calls in the morning.

DAVID: Me, too.

ANDREW: I have a couple of appointments— A couple of interviews. A class to teach—

DAVID: Sure.

ANDREW: I suppose Margaret can take it.

(ANDREW *puts his head in his hands.* DAVID *comes to* ANDREW *and holds him.*)

DAVID: You can give me the tour of beautiful Dixon, Illinois.

ANDREW: I'll give you the tour.

DAVID: I want to go through Reagan's house.

ANDREW: It's boring.

DAVID: I want to leave droppings. Please?

ANDREW: Yeh.

DAVID: And introduce me to the old lady?

ANDREW: God. Promise to still like me—

DAVID: What?

ANDREW: Promise. No matter what. To still like me.

DAVID: Boy Scout Honor.

ANDREW: Okay.

(*Music. The lights crossfade to* TOMMY *and* CHUCK *who are in the kitchen of his home. They sit at table. There is a beer bottle in front of* TOMMY *and* CHUCK. *It's morning.*)

TOMMY: So I get called at two in the morning! Two in the morning. And it's Lorna Utter asking me to come right over "to the Reagan House". The pipes have burst and the basement is flooding—

CHUCK: Jesus Christ.

TOMMY: Exactly what I'm thinking—and so I say in this fog I'm in, I say—Lorna, what the hell are you doing at the Reagan Home at two in the morning and what in God's name are you doing in the basement? She tells me she always goes there when she can't sleep and she does touch up painting on the rooms. She's painting around the front door in the hall and she hears water running. Turns out it's a broken pipe and can I get right over because it's "an historical emergency". I'm telling you I should have never volunteered to work the place. Never. But I get out of bed and go on over and get the water turned off and get back to bed at the three. I was not polite to Lorna.

CHUCK: I'm glad you came over.

TOMMY: Why wouldn't I come over, Chuck?

CHUCK: I got all wound up.

TOMMY: *(looking into box)* So he's not doing so well?

CHUCK: What do you think his problem is?

TOMMY: He's tired.

CHUCK: That's all?

TOMMY: How old is he?

CHUCK: Seventeen.

TOMMY: He's real tired.

CHUCK: I got home from work this morning and he's just lying there. I thought at first he was dead. And then I put my head down to his little body and just listened a while to his breathing, picked him and took him to bed with me and talked to him. I couldn't sleep so I got up, thought may be I should put him in this box and take him to the vet. That's when I called you.

TOMMY: You ought to take him in.

CHUCK: Think so?

TOMMY: It's time he was put to sleep.

CHUCK: You think it's that bad?

TOMMY: I think you should take him in. I think you should have a vet take a look at him.

CHUCK: I don't know if I can put him to sleep. I've had this guy for so long. You think he's that bad?

TOMMY: That's my best advice.

CHUCK: I don't know if I can do that. What if they say it's time? I don't know if I can do it. Poor thing. Poor old thing. He's my buddy.

TOMMY: I've never seen a man take to a cat like you take to this one.

CHUCK: Well, I do.

TOMMY: I know you do—

CHUCK: I love this old thing.

TOMMY: Well, you're not doing him any favors.

CHUCK: Do you think he's in pain?

TOMMY: He's not moved since I started looking at him so I think he might be in some kind of pain.

CHUCK: *(To the box)* Are you in pain, Smiley? Do you hurt, little baby?

TOMMY: He's not going to answer you.

CHUCK: I know that. But the sound of my voice. It makes him feel better.

TOMMY: You're going to have to give that up. The cat's dying and that's all there is to it.

CHUCK: Shut up.

TOMMY: I'm sorry, but he is.

CHUCK: I don't need you to tell me that.

TOMMY: It seems to me—

CHUCK: I said shut up. I know what's happening.

TOMMY: You don't have to get mad at me.

CHUCK: I'm upset. My cat's dying and I'm very upset.

TOMMY: I ought to go home.

CHUCK: You don't have to leave.

TOMMY: Seems to me like—

CHUCK: I'm sorry.

TOMMY: Well—

CHUCK: My cat's sick. That's all.

TOMMY: Well, I'm just trying to help.

CHUCK: I know that and I'm sorry. I didn't mean to snap your head off.

TOMMY: Well—

CHUCK: I should call Jan.

TOMMY: You should call Jan.

CHUCK: Ask her what I should do.

TOMMY: Call her then.

CHUCK: What if she says to put him to sleep?

TOMMY: Then you'll have to do it.

CHUCK: Do you think I should?

TOMMY: I think he's sick.

CHUCK: Should I cover him?

TOMMY: The cat's sick.

CHUCK: I'll cover him with this.

TOMMY: He's probably cold.

CHUCK: *(With towel)* Here you go, little guy. Little pal. Here you go, you little cutie pie, little thing you.

TOMMY: Your dad's going to take care you.

CHUCK: That's right. That's right.

TOMMY: If I didn't see it with my own eyes.

CHUCK: What's that?

TOMMY: You. Mooning over a cat.

CHUCK: His name's Smiley.

TOMMY: When I was just a kid—you remember me? I was a bone. A bone of a kid and we had this big cat, a twenty pounder. Rudy was his name. Big thing. Big old thing. Anyway, I woke up in the middle of the night and here's this cat with his paws locked around my throat and his mouth up against my mouth sucking the air out of my lungs. Scared the hell out of me. And so I grabbed hold of him by the throat and I flung him off of me and up against the bedroom wall.

CHUCK: You shouldn't have done that.

TOMMY: He never tried it again and that's for sure—

CHUCK: You're just plain mean, you know it?

TOMMY: He tried to kill me. He was strangling me.

CHUCK: Cats don't choke people.

TOMMY: Well, this one did. A strange, sick cat if you want to know. With a strange, sick hold over my mother. I'd come home from school and there she'd be—sitting at the kitchen table, petting that cat, staring into space like she and Rudy were on some kind of mind trip together. The two of them sitting there smoking cigarettes—

CHUCK: Bullshit.

TOMMY: I'm telling you that fucking cat smoked. My mom would put the cigarette down to his lips and he'd take a drag.

CHUCK: *(Simultaneous to above)* Bullshit. Bullshit.

TOMMY: He could blow smoke rings, for Christ sake! And he coughed just like my mom. A hacking cough. A terrible, terrible cough that comes from one place and that's smoking. *(He does a loud cat cough.)* And then he'd try to catch his breath like this. *(He gasps and chokes loudly.)*

CHUCK: *(To cat)* You hear this guy? You hear this bullshitter? *(Suddenly)* He's looking up.

TOMMY: Lets see.

CHUCK: He's better, I think. You feeling better? Huh? Don't lean in so close.

TOMMY: I'm just looking.

CHUCK: Well, I don't want you to scare him.

TOMMY: I'm not scaring him. I don't think I was scaring him.

CHUCK: He knows when you don't like him. He's not an idiot.

TOMMY: But he's a cat.

CHUCK: They have an instinct!

TOMMY: But he's still a cat. A cat.

CHUCK: I know.

TOMMY: An animal.

CHUCK: I know that. But you scared my sick cat.

TOMMY: I didn't—

CHUCK: Looked like you did.

TOMMY: Well, I did not!

(Silence. Then)

CHUCK: Sorry. I don't want to hurt your feelings.

TOMMY: Well—

CHUCK: I'm gonna mesh his food right now. Is that okay?

TOMMY: Meshing food might make him eat.

CHUCK: I think if I make it soft enough. Maybe I should spoon feed him.

TOMMY: You could try that...so how's Jan doing?

CHUCK: Okay.

TOMMY: Okay?

CHUCK: She's doing okay. I've talked to her twice this morning already. And she sounds okay.

TOMMY: Twice?

CHUCK: Well, she left the place in such a mess. I can't find anything. And I've got these electric and these gas bills and I'm looking at them like what the hell is this! She couldn't take care of this before she left?!

TOMMY: You don't get mad at her, do you?

CHUCK: I don't get mad.

TOMMY: Well, don't... Does she still come by to make you supper?

CHUCK: Yes.

TOMMY: That's a nice thing.

CHUCK: It is nice.

TOMMY: Boy, you know , call me crazy, but I think she still loves you.

CHUCK: She doesn't love me.

TOMMY: Why would she leave you then keep coming back every night to fix your supper?

CHUCK: And she does a load of laundry.

TOMMY: She can't get enough of you.

CHUCK: I don't know. I hadn't thought about it.

TOMMY: She still loves you.

CHUCK: Then why did she leave me?

TOMMY: I don't know...that's what this is, you know? The cat. Your worry about the cat. It's Jan.

CHUCK: I thought you said it was because I was— *(He does the gesture.)*

TOMMY: I was kidding. That girl still loves you. She's just got a crazy streak in her, that's all.... Do you remember the day Jan started chasing those boys with an ax?

CHUCK: She was protecting her brother.

TOMMY: What was his name?

CHUCK: Andy. Andrew.

TOMMY: That's it. Andy. Andrew. *(He laughs.)* Don't tell Jan this, but it was my parents who called the police. Jan is a great girl, a smart girl, but I know she broke your heart—and I know she can swing a mean ax. She's got that in her.

CHUCK: She does.

TOMMY: And that's why I'm saying she still loves you. She has an unstable side that makes her walk out on you even when she still cares for you.

CHUCK: You think so?

TOMMY: I know so. I'm sure so.

CHUCK: He's sniffing!! He's licking it!

TOMMY: He's a good boy.

CHUCK: Keep licking, sweetie. Good boy. Good Smiley.

TOMMY: Yea...I'm sorry about...

CHUCK: I know that.

TOMMY: I wasn't trying to scare—

CHUCK: I didn't think you were—

TOMMY: I'm worried for you. You're worried, I'm worried, you know?

CHUCK: I know.

TOMMY: Your wife leaves you, you look depressed, you lose weight, you get hypnotized by your cat, a friend has to get worried. He has to.

(Beat)

CHUCK: She still loves me?

TOMMY: I can't see any other way.

CHUCK: Did you hear that kitty? Mama still loves us. Yea....

(As the lights crossfade to a bed in a nursing home. MAE lies in the bed, singing Jambalayas. *JAN sits at her side.)*

MAE: Why don't you sing with me?

JAN: You don't want me to sing with you.

MAE: Yes, I do.

JAN: You never have before.

MAE: I do now.

JAN: I can't sing.

MAE: Everybody can sing.

JAN: Not me.

MAE: You could if you tried.

JAN: I don't know the words.

MAE: I've been singing that song for a hundred years and you don't know the words?

(MAE *and* JAN *sing a little of the song.*)

MAE: That's not bad.

JAN: Yes, it is.

MAE: No, it was pretty. They've asked me to sing for the recreation hour this morning.

JAN: I heard.

MAE: I told them I would have to think about it. I told them I would have to check my voice. "But we love the way you sing. We've heard you sing. Our parents" —get that— "our parents heard you sing. Everyone has heard Mae Pierce sing." Then they start talking about me singing for President Reagan that one time—

JAN: Well, you were a big hit.

MAE: I was a big hit—and Ronny couldn't take his off of me.

JAN: So you say.

MAE: I do say. I do say. And that skinny bitch of his—

JAN: Mom—

MAE: There's not one person in this country doesn't think—

JAN: It isn't—

MAE: It is. It is. It is. She was jealous and everybody knew that, too. Tried to stab me in the back with her comments. I'm prettier than her and everybody knows that. Including Ronny—

JAN: Ronny—

MAE: I call him Ronny. In my head. When he comes dancing in my head late at night.

JAN: Well, you should do it. It'll make you feel better. I noticed you've got your best robe on.

MAE: And this underneath.

JAN: That's a nice combo. And your makeup is pretty.

MAE: Is it too exotic? I don't want to look Oriental.

JAN: You don't.

MAE: I suppose I should do it although I don't feel much like singing, really. And what am I going to sing? And does anybody in this place still have their hearing—

JAN: Mom.

MAE: Well, it's true. I can't mince words, you know that. Is that all you're going to do?

JAN: I have to get this done.

MAE: Give them all "A"s.

JAN: Mmm.

MAE: Just throw them all away, go into class and tell them "Surprise you all got 'A's!"

JAN: They would be surprised.

MAE: "A"s from mean, old Mrs Williamson.

(*Beat.* JAN *looks at* MAE.)

MAE: I hear what they say. I know your reputation.

(*Beat*)

MAE: Is that what you wear when you teach?

JAN: Something like this, yes.

MAE: I think you should try more color.

JAN: I think this is fine.

MAE: I think you should try something brighter.
The kids like color, they like brightness. You dress
like a tree.

JAN: I beg your pardon.

MAE: *(A little louder)* I said you dress like a tree—

JAN: I dress fine—

MAE: You would be so much more popular with your
students if wore a little brightness!! You wear some
bright reds or yellows or blues and those kids will
gather around you like little bees. Like little—
(She waves her hand.) —bees! Like little—what are
those things—they like color—and they buzz around—
and they drive me crazy—quick little things—
hummingbirds!!

JAN: When have you ever seen a hummingbird?

MAE: I've seen a lot of hummingbirds. They're just
naturally attracted to me. All my bright colors. No one
would ever mistake me for a tree!

JAN: I dress the way I want to, which I think is just fine.

(Beat)

MAE: You don't have to jump all over me.

JAN: I wasn't—

MAE: I'm giving you suggestions. That's all I'm doing.
I'm a mother and mothers should give suggestions.
(Beat) Are you just going to sit there and grade papers?

JAN: Do you want to do something?

MAE: Can't think of what to do. What is that?

JAN: Essays on the poetry of Robert Frost.

MAE: Sounds awful. *(As she sings again.)* I haven't decided to sing, yet.

JAN: They said you were real excited when they asked you.

MAE: I might. I might not. It depends.

JAN: On what?

MAE: If I've got the mood or not. I might not have the mood and if I don't have the mood, I'm not moving from this bed. I don't know why Andy's not here.

JAN: He'll be here.

MAE: I thought he'd call by now. Tell us he was here.

JAN: Do you want to get out of bed?

MAE: No.

JAN: Why don't you get out of bed and come have a cigarette with me?

MAE: I don't want a cigarette.

JAN: You need to get some exercise.

MAE: I don't feel like getting out of bed.

JAN: I feel like a cigarette.

MAE: Go have one then. I won't stop you.

JAN: Why don't you walk out with me?

MAE: Is there a sun?

JAN: It's very sunny.

MAE: I don't like the sun. It hurts my eyes.

JAN: Use my sunglasses. Come on now. Get out of bed.

MAE: I need a wheelchair.

JAN: You can walk.

MAE: Not today. Today, I need a wheelchair.

JAN: You want me to call a nurse?

MAE: They'll never come. It takes forever.

JAN: So what do you want to do?

MAE: I want to lie here and take a nap. Leave me alone.

JAN: All right. *(She begins to grade her papers.)*

MAE: Are there anymore of those cherry chocolates in the drawer?

JAN: They're sitting right beside you.

MAE: Oh, there they are. Would you get me one?

JAN: You can't reach them?

MAE: You can't get me one?

(JAN gets her a cherry chocolate.)

JAN: Here you go.

MAE: Some of these are missing.

JAN: There are?

MAE: One, two, three, four, five. Last night I had eight.

JAN: You ate more than you thought.

MAE: I had eight when I went to bed. It's that weird woman I told you about. She steals things from me.

JAN: Nobody's stealing things from you.

MAE: She steals my cherry chocolates and my cigarettes.

JAN: Why don't you tell the nurse?

MAE: Why don't you? You're my daughter. You should be protecting me. Somebody should be protecting me.

JAN: I'll say something.

MAE: Don't bother. It wouldn't do any good—

JAN: I'll talk to a nurse.

MAE: A lot of good that will do. The crazy old bag just wanders around this place—in one room and out the other—taking stuff as she pleases. I wake up from a little nap and there she is standing right in front of me with a fistful of my cigarettes and I say to her "Listen, you old bag, keep your hands off my cigarettes and my cherry chocolates or I'll shoot you dead, you crazy bitch."

JAN: Don't use—

MAE: And I then I raise my hand underneath my covers to look like I have a gun—

(NORMA, an old woman, comes to door.)

MAE: That's her!

JAN: (To old woman) Hi, can I help you?

(The old woman turns abruptly and leaves.)

MAE: Do you see? Do you see?

JAN: She looks harmless.

MAE: She's crazy. What am I doing in a place for crazy people? You put me in a nut house to recuperate from a broken ankle? This is as good as you can do?

JAN: This is a nursing home, not a—and the doctor says—

MAE: Some doctor.

JAN: You should get up and walk everyday.

MAE: Or else he'll cut off my foot.

JAN: He's not going to cut off your foot.

MAE: He'll cut off my foot! That's what he does to people who don't do what he says! He cuts off their feet! (She begins to cry.) I don't know what's wrong with me. I have nothing to look forward to. Nothing. You sit

there, you grade papers. You won't let me help.
I can't do it anymore. I want a cherry chocolate.

JAN: Here you go.

(Grabbing JAN's *arm)*

MAE: I'd like a drink.

JAN: You can't have a drink.

MAE: But I'd like one.

JAN: Well, forget it.

MAE: You could sneak one in.

JAN: I'm not doing that.

MAE: How about one vodka martini?

JAN: No.

MAE: Well, thanks for nothing!

JAN: You're welcome.

(Beat)

MAE: Where is Andy? He said he'd be here today. You
bore me, you know that. You just bore me to death.

JAN: Then I'll leave.

MAE: Oh, no. No. I'm sorry.

JAN: You want me to leave?

MAE: No. I'm sorry.... *(Picking up the box of chocolates)*
Would you like a cherry chocolate?

(Beat)

JAN: All right. Thanks.

MAE: Eat all you want.

JAN: One should do it.

MAE: But you can have all you want.

JAN: One is enough. What are all these labels?

MAE: The nurse brought them to me.

JAN: What are you doing with them?

MAE: They're for you and Andy. I want you to go to my house, pick out the things you want, write your name on the label and then put it on the item.

JAN: Why would I do that?

MAE: So when I die there won't be any argument.

JAN: You're not dying—

MAE: Take the labels.

JAN: You think Andrew and I are going to fight over—

MAE: I want you to do this.

JAN: There's nothing I want.

MAE: Nothing?

JAN: I just said that.

MAE: There is nothing of mine that you want?

JAN: No.

MAE: You are such a bitch to me.

JAN: Don't use that word—

MAE: You are such a bitch—

JAN: I hate that word—

MAE: There is nothing you want?

JAN: Give me some labels.

MAE: *(Handing them to her)* Put them on everything you think you might want. *(Beat. She begins to sing* I Walk the Line.*)*

JAN: *(Over* MAE*'s singing)* You know if you exercised more, you'd feel better. The nurses say that you're

doing pretty well in physical therapy, but they can't
get you to move once they bring you back to the room.
If you'd get out of bed and walk, you might get well.

MAE: I have no place to walk. I have no place to go.
I don't want to just wander. I don't like that. I look
at those people in the halls—and that's all they do.
They wander. They wander down the east wing,
they wander down the west wing. They keep their
heads down and wander like they're following some
kind of yellow line that's supposed to lead them out
of here. Keep your eye on the yellow line and the next
time you look up—the next time you have the strength
to raise your head, you'll be free. Can I go home? I want
to go home.

JAN: When your ankle is strong.

MAE: And when will that be?

JAN: When you get out of bed. When you start to
move around.

MAE: The social worker says I've a low grade
depression. Is that true? Do I have a low grade
depression?

JAN: I think you might.

MAE: I've never been depressed in my life.

JAN: I think you might be now.

MAE: I'm tired.

JAN: You're depressed, too.

MAE: I should be depressed at this stage in my life.

JAN: Mmm, maybe.

MAE: I have good reason to be depressed. I wheel
myself down to the lunch room and look out over the
tables and there's a sea of depression lapping up at my
feet. And the nurses want me to sit in the middle of

that, they want me to eat in the middle of all that depression, surrounded by a mess of depressed fish that you keep seeing over and over and over again, their little mouths bobbing at the top, moving their lips like this. *(She does a fish imitation.)* They're like this. *(She does fish imitation again.)*

JAN: They are not—

MAE: Some of them are like this. *(She does imitation again.)* They eat then sink to the bottom. *(Beat)* Nothing's going right.

JAN: I know.

MAE: I have a whole lot of problems.

JAN: You do.

MAE: I had a major operation. I get put into a nursing home. I have a son who won't visit— *(Beat)* Help me up here. I want to walk. I want to walk down the halls.

(Crossfade to the lobby of the nursing home. ANDREW stands there waiting as DAVID enters.)

DAVID: She's in 214, Hall B.

ANDREW: Oh.

DAVID: Should we go in?

ANDREW: I'm not ready, yet. Do you mind? If we just sit. For a minute.

DAVID: I don't mind.

ANDREW: Just for a minute. I have to gear up for this. I have to figure out what I'm going to say.

DAVID: Okay.

ANDREW: Thanks. *(Beat)* You can see my grade school from here.

DAVID: Where is it?

ANDREW: There. Behind the trees. The courthouse is there. That clump of trees hides a statue of Lincoln—on a horse, galloping somewhere or other. A log cabin behind him. That's the roof of Reagan's boyhood home—

DAVID: Where?

ANDREW: Right through there. A bus has probably just pulled up and a group of students is pouring out and into the house, I would imagine. I would imagine... well...

DAVID: You're all right?

ANDREW: It's been a long time.

DAVID: But you're doing okay?

ANDREW: I suppose so. We used to come here and sing for the old folks. Used to sing Christmas carols. Strange...we would line up in the cafeteria and the residents would gather around us like we might be something good to eat. Weird. Strange.

DAVID: I'll bet.

ANDREW: I'm not crazy about what it's doing to me. I don't feel good about this. I feel...small suddenly. Very small. And a little embarrassed.

DAVID: You're with me.

ANDREW: That's why I'm embarrassed. I don't like you to see me like this.

DAVID: It's okay.

ANDREW: I shouldn't have talked to Jan like I did.

DAVID: You were rude.

ANDREW: She never did anything to me. Never. I suppose she's here. I suppose I should apologize.

DAVID: Where's your house from here?

ANDREW: You can't see it. But it's in through there. The trees are in the way....

DAVID: Maybe we'll drive by.

ANDREW: Yea.

DAVID: I'd like to see it.

ANDREW: Maybe.

DAVID: I'll drive really quickly.

ANDREW: I don't know. I'm not real sure—

DAVID: You're so hunched over.

ANDREW: That's what I mean.

DAVID: What?

ANDREW: This place has shrunk me a few inches. I go to the gym everyday just to keep this from happening, but I can see it's done me no good. *(Mimicking)* I'm melting. I'm melting...what should I say when I see her?

DAVID: Who?

ANDREW: My mother.

DAVID: What do you want to say?

ANDREW: Oh, God, I don't know. I'd thought for awhile that my entire childhood was a figment of my imagination and then Jan calls. Things were going fine, weren't they? Weren't they going fine?

DAVID: Yes.

ANDREW: Things were fine.

DAVID: Things were fine.

ANDREW: What do you think I should say?

DAVID: What do you want to say?

ANDREW: Nothing.

DAVID: Really?

ANDREW: I can't think of anything. In fact, I can barely picture the scene in my head. And what I do picture is me standing at the foot of her bed, head down, silent. I'm mostly scared right now.

DAVID: I'll take her down.

ANDREW: Will you?

DAVID: If she gets rough.

ANDREW: That I would like to see.

DAVID: I can handle mothers.

ANDREW: She's pretty fierce.

DAVID: Me, too. One thing to remember. *(Whispering)* I love you.

(DAVID reaches for him.)

ANDREW: *(Standing)* Oh. Good. Good. Okay... I look at a place like this and it blows my whole theory on life. Does anything about life really matter if you finish it here— wandering the halls of a nursing home? Live your life to the fullest so that you can someday end it with a glazed eyed lack of memory.

DAVID: Perhaps there's some peace in that kind of existence.

ANDREW: Really, you think so?

DAVID: I don't know for sure, but I know my grandfather ended up that way. And he was this larger then life socialist agitator who picked up the world with his bare hands and literally wrung it dry. Like this. *(He does a movement. And then the voice)*. David, he'd say! You must fight for the masses!!! And I'd say Yes! Grandpa!! Bring me the blood of a capitalist! He'd flip out if he had to sit and look at these pictures of Reagan everywhere.

ANDREW: Be careful what you say. He was a hometown boy.

DAVID: He'd pull himself up, *(Standing)* look the guy straight in the eye and holler out, "You, sir" —sir because grandpa was always a gentleman— "were bad for the Jews!!"

ANDREW: Shhhh.

DAVID: But he was bad for the Jews. Some Jews, anyway. The good Jews.

ANDREW: Sit.

DAVID: No one even looked our way.

ANDREW: The man in the wheelchair hasn't taken his eyes off of us.

DAVID: Trust me, he hasn't noticed us.

ANDREW: God.

DAVID: What?

ANDREW: You'll kill me before you put me in a nursing home, won't you?

DAVID: I'll hire someone.

ANDREW: I'm serious, David. I don't want to be put in a nursing home. Promise me. Promise me right now. If you can't take care of me, you'll off me somehow.

DAVID: I'll off you somehow.

ANDREW: I mean it.

DAVID: I mean it, too. I'll push you out a window.

ANDREW: How bad will I have to be?

DAVID: What do you mean?

ANDREW: Before you kill me?

DAVID: Pretty bad.

ANDREW: How bad?

DAVID: ...Pretty bad.

ANDREW: In a wheelchair like that guy?

DAVID: Yes.

ANDREW: What if I can still feed myself and go to the bathroom?

DAVID: You can't dance or go shopping?

ANDREW: No, I just sit there like that guy.

DAVID: I'd still kill you.

ANDREW: You're not taking any of this seriously.

DAVID: No, I'm not.

ANDREW: But I think we should talk about this.

DAVID: Because we're in a nursing home?

ANDREW: Because we've never talked about it before.

DAVID: It's a little premature, don't you think?

ANDREW: Not if I'm thinking about it.

DAVID: Well, I'm not thinking about it. When we get home, write it all down and put it in a safe deposit box. When you get dementia—which I'm sure you will— I'll open the box and carry out all of your wishes.

ANDREW: *(Seriously)* Thank you... Will you cremate my body?

DAVID: Jews don't cremate.

ANDREW: But I want to be cremated.

DAVID: Marry a protestant. Ever heard of the holocaust? I don't do cremations. The body goes back the way it was found. That's a Jewish thing.

ANDREW: So you won't go through with my wishes.

DAVID: No.

ANDREW: I'm a helpless dead person and yet you wouldn't go through with my wishes?

DAVID: All right. Lets pretend for a minute that you're dead.*(Pause. He closes his eyes.)* Okay. Now you're dead. And, okay, so I have you cremated.

ANDREW: Thank you...I want a small service by the lake. Invite all our friends. Say something really nice.

DAVID: That will be hard.

ANDREW: It will?

DAVID: I'm kidding you, Andrew.

ANDREW: Oh...what will you say?

DAVID: I don't know.

ANDREW: No idea?

DAVID: I don't have one fucking idea.

ANDREW: Are you kidding?

DAVID: You really think I should have figured out your eulogy?

ANDREW: It just seems like it should pop into your head.

DAVID: Well, it doesn't.

ANDREW: Oh...seems like it should.

DAVID: It doesn't.

ANDREW: Oh...I have a eulogy for you.

DAVID: What?

ANDREW: I know what I'm going to say when you die.

DAVID: You're joking?

ANDREW: I've thought about losing you. I've thought about it. *(Taking out his wallet)* See what I have here.

DAVID: What is it?

ANDREW: *(Reading from a piece of paper)* "In case of emergency, call David Sabin at home: 404-1132 or work: 728-9177". So if something happens, you'll be the first to know.

DAVID: You're so depressing.

ANDREW: Am I?

DAVID: Today, yes, you're depressing.

ANDREW: I think about it. I worry about it. I go to work, I ride the train and I begin to think about what if something happens to me and I don't make it home. What will happen to David? What will he think? Shouldn't he know immediately? And who else do I have, huh? Who else? ...I think you should do the same.

DAVID: As soon we get home.

ANDREW: I don't want to be waiting. If you're killed, I want to know. I want someone to call me. That way I can start immediately making funeral arrangements—

DAVID: Oh, God—

ANDREW: And memorizing the eulogy which I have already begun to prepare.

DAVID: Are you kidding me? I cannot believe it. You're nuts, you know it. You're crazy—

ANDREW: *(Overlapping)* And I'm going to say something about how meeting you saved my life.

DAVID: What?

ANDREW: You heard me.

DAVID: No, I didn't.

ANDREW: Well, I won't say it again.

DAVID: I saved your life. What? Really?

ANDREW: Yes.

DAVID: I didn't know.

ANDREW: You did.

DAVID: *(As he leans into him)* I truly didn't know—

ANDREW: *(Jerking away)* Does it smell in here? I think it smells in here? I think it smells like *(Whispering)* urine? Is that a urine smell?...I think it smells like *(Whispering)* shit or something. *(He stands up and sniffs.)* It does. It smells like *(Whispering)* feces. It smells like *(Whispering)* shit. What kind of a nursing home is this?

DAVID: One that smells like shit. Sit down.

ANDREW: But is that right? Does that seem right to you? Don't they clean in here? Have they never heard of Pinesol?

DAVID: I don't know.

ANDREW: Pinesol would get rid of the odor. *(Beat)* Or Lysol. Lysol does it, too.

DAVID: Go buy some Pinesol—or Lysol and start scrubbing.

ANDREW: What am I doing here, anyway? I said I'd never come back. You heard me say it.

DAVID: I heard you.

ANDREW: And what nerve, you know? My sister calling me in the middle of the night. Like it's an emergency.

DAVID: So she wanted to—

ANDREW: And leaving messages. How many messages did she leave?

DAVID: About fifteen hundred.

ANDREW: She's the one who decided to stay here. She didn't have to stay. It's not like Mom was any better to

her. You should have heard the way Mom talked to her.
You should have seen some of the things she had to
do because Mom couldn't cope. And now suddenly I
should care? I should care about any of this?

DAVID: Would you slow down—

ANDREW: And why is my name and work number not
in your billfold?

(DAVID *takes his hand.* ANDREW *jerks away.*)

ANDREW: Don't do that. Don't hold my hand here.

DAVID: What?

ANDREW: Don't hold my hand here. This isn't the place.

DAVID: This isn't the place?

ANDREW: No.

DAVID: What place, then?

ANDREW: Not here, that's all.

DAVID: You're a lunatic.

ANDREW: I'm a lunatic, fine. Just don't come back to my
hometown expecting to hold my hand.

(DAVID *looks at him as* ANDREW *turns away as the lights
crossfade to* TOMMY *and* CHUCK. *There are two more beer
bottles in front of* TOMMY.)

TOMMY: Terrible.

CHUCK: I know.

TOMMY: Terrible, terrible.

CHUCK: I know it was.

TOMMY: What a situation. When I was a kid every time
we'd drive by their house, my old lady would say
"saddest house in town". Every time. "Saddest house
in town." "This is the saddest house in town." This and
that and this and that and saddest house in town.

CHUCK: It was sad.

TOMMY: Jan's little sister dies.

CHUCK: It was terrible.

TOMMY: Then her dad. Think about it.

CHUCK: Terrible stuff, no doubt.

TOMMY: Nice man, too.

CHUCK: He was quiet, I remember.

TOMMY: My parents used to go to Jimmy's to hear the old lady sing.

CHUCK: Mine would never—

TOMMY: They said she was always half-drunk by the time the night was out—

CHUCK: I heard that, too.

TOMMY: *(Continuing)* —telling off colored jokes— she was a dirty old thing, that I heard.

CHUCK: But she can sing.

TOMMY: Then marrying Jimmy—

CHUCK: That was something.

TOMMY: Raising a family like two drunks on a pogo stick.

CHUCK: But Jan did all right.

TOMMY: She took care of things. Took care of that nutty family.

CHUCK: She did that.

TOMMY: She did.

CHUCK: And it got to her. It gets to her still.

TOMMY: Exactly.

CHUCK: There's been a few times, she's locked herself in the bathroom. Sometimes for two or three hours and always in the middle of the night.

TOMMY: You're kidding.

CHUCK: So I stand outside saying: Open the door! I'm your husband!

TOMMY: Exactly. You're the husband. With an emphasis on you're and husband.

CHUCK: She wouldn't come out until I'd gone to work—

TOMMY: That's instability. She has a general instability. You should call her, Chuck. You call her. You ask about Smiley. You say he's real sick. You ask her what should you do.

CHUCK: Okay.

TOMMY: Then I would ask "Are you coming by tonight to make my supper".

CHUCK: She always does though.

TOMMY: So she'll say yes and you'll say "Why do you do that, Jan? Why do you come over every night to make my supper?"

CHUCK: She straightens up a little, too.

TOMMY: She's crazy about you.

CHUCK: Yea.

TOMMY: She is. You know, Chuck, it may be menopausal, that's all. It may be strictly menopausal. My wife is menopausal right now and it's driving me nuts. In fact, I wish she would leave, you know? Cook my supper and then leave.

CHUCK: That bad, huh?

TOMMY: She's hot; she's cold. She's hot; she's cold.
It was menopause that turned her into a Jehovah's
Witness.

CHUCK: You think so?

TOMMY: I'm sure so. I say, honey, why this—why the
Jehovah's Witness and you know what she does?

CHUCK: What?

TOMMY: Just stares at me like I got fire coming out of
my head. "Put Satan behind you", she says.

CHUCK: Satan?

TOMMY: That's right.

CHUCK: I didn't know she'd gotten that bad.

TOMMY: I can't get within ten feet of her.

CHUCK: So you think Jan is going through menopause?

TOMMY: I think there's a chance, yes, I do.

CHUCK: I don't know.

TOMMY: What?

CHUCK: Jan's pretty distant with me—

TOMMY: That's menopause.

CHUCK: Like I'm not there. When she told me she was
leaving, she barely moved. She didn't blink an eye.
Liked she'd practiced or something. Like it'd been years
of thinking and planning. Years. I built her this brand
new kitchen. Look at the place. She says she wants
ceramic tiles; I put in tile. Look at this stuff: like a
golden sidewalk, for Christ sake! Like a sheik lives
here or something. The floor alone cost five thousand
dollars—

TOMMY: (Overlapping) I helped put it in. I know!

CHUCK: I do everything she asks. I say where do you want the stove? She says "put it over there" and so I put it over there. And look at this stove. There are so many gadgets and goofas—

TOMMY: You're a goofas—

CHUCK: —and computer chips chipping away inside the thing that she could practically fly the son of a bitch to the moon! She could run the universe! She could reshape and remake the laws of physics. Solve the problems of the world. Make visits to the Pope. Go to Hollywood and meet some movie star— And the whole time sucken the air out of my backside—my aching backside. Now I have Smiley here, dying on me, slipping out the back door like my daughter in college, like my wife in some tiny apartment without any furniture. Years, she planned this. Saved up for it, I know. Years. She even planned to quit her teaching position without telling me. The whole thing mapped out for herself. This is the reason she comes back to cook for me. She misses this kitchen; this space ship; this Sheik's paradise! I'm telling you, Tommy, I want to die! I just want to die. Just die.

TOMMY: You stop talking like that—

(CHUCK *picks up box with Smiley*)

CHUCK: I ought to take him in, I ought to just take control and say "This is it. Gas him."

TOMMY: I'm telling you now, you stop that talk. Pull yourself up, pick up the phone and call her. I'll stand by you.

CHUCK: Yea?

TOMMY: Go to the phone—

CHUCK: She's at the nursing home.

TOMMY: Call the nursing home—Put the box down.

(CHUCK *puts the box on the floor.*)

TOMMY: Now make your call.

(CHUCK *picks up the phone. The lights cross fade to* JAN *and* MAE *who are walking up and down the hallway.*)

JAN: This feels good, doesn't it?

MAE: It's okay. It's rocky going.

JAN: You're doing great. You're doing better than I thought you would.

MAE: Can we go to the patio?

JAN: Yes.

MAE: I want to look out the window. I want to see if Andrew has come. I want to wait for him.

JAN: We can do that.

(Silence. They walk for a bit.)

MAE: I can't stand the way some of these people look. Do I look like that? Do I look that poorly?

JAN: No, you don't.

MAE: I will if you keep me here. A month, a week, one more day even and I'll be just like that. *(To another patient)* What are you looking at, honey? I'm just walking. People walk up and down this hall all day. There's nothing special about it. Just keep your eyes to the floor, keep your eyes on the yellow line—

JAN: Mom.

MAE: There's part of the problem. These people have lost their minds. I've still got a mind. I can still think clearly. This is not a place for me. These people don't remember that they're going to die. But I remember! Did you see her staring at me? Gives me the creeps. Makes me very nervous. I'm not sure I'm even safe here with that kind of woman. Unless they tie her down at night who knows what she might do while I'm sleeping. I could be murdered. I could be strangled. You could choke that bitch to death and she wouldn't know what was happening to her. *(To invisible woman)* I could choke you to death and it wouldn't even phase you, would it?! But I'd know. I'd know I was going to die. *(Beat)* How far is the patio, anyway? I thought it was just down the hall.

JAN: Hall D.

MAE: Hall D? I can't go all the way down to hall D. This is only hall B. Hall B! How long, oh Lord, how long must I suffer? *(To another patient)* What are you staring at? You know, honey, I wish I could be oblivious just like you.

JAN: Stop it, Mom—

MAE: I want to be drifting off somewhere just like you, sweetie. I don't want to recognize anyone.

JAN: Would you stop it!?

MAE: I don't want to know where I am. I don't want to be aware of what's happening to me. I like the idea of crying for no reason. Shouting for no reason. Laughing for no reason. And staring right back at you. *(To patient)* That's very rude, staring at people like that—

JAN: Shhhh.

MAE: Oh my God, we have so far to go. I can't do it. I just can't do it. How long, oh Lord, how long?

JAN: Oh, stop with the religion stuff—

MAE: I'm religious.

JAN: *(Laughing)* You are not religious. You're suspicious. You're superstitious, but you are not religious!

MAE: The way you talk to me!

JAN: And the way you talk!

(MAE *suddenly freezes in her tracks.*)

JAN: What are you doing? *(Beat)* I said what are you doing?

(Beat. MAE *begins to recite The Lord's Prayer.)*

JAN: Mom.

(Beat. MAE *continues reciting until her next line.)*

JAN: Mom? *(Beat)* This is ridiculous. *(Beat)* Everybody knows "The Lord's Prayer", Mother. That doesn't mean anything. *(Beat)* I'm going back to the room. *(Beat)* You want me to leave you here? *(Beat)* You're just like them, Mother. Crazy just like them. *(She starts to walk away.)* I'm going back to the room. *(She walks a bit further.)* Mom?

MAE: *(Suddenly stopping her recitation)* Do you have any idea how angry I am? Do you have any idea at all?

(MAE *starts to walk past* JAN *who stands there a beat as lights crossfade to* DAVID *and* ANDREW. ANDREW *turns and looks at* DAVID.)

DAVID: You're going to sit over there?

ANDREW: Yes.

DAVID: You're going to sit over there?

ANDREW: Yes. Right here. I going to sit right here.

DAVID: Jesus.

ANDREW: What? I can't sit over here? I can't sit where I want?

DAVID: I'm coming over.

ANDREW: Don't.

DAVID: I'm coming.

ANDREW: Shut up.

DAVID: Here I come.

ANDREW: *(As* DAVID, *acting like a very weird old person, moves over to him)* Stop it. Stop it.

DAVID: *(As old person)* Take my hand. Hold my hand, sonny, honey. I just want to hold your hand. Let me hold your hand.

ANDREW: *(Overlapping)* Don't do that. David. Don't.

DAVID: *(As himself)* You're embarrassed, you're scared, you're repulsed? What? What?

ANDREW: No. This isn't the place—why do I have to explain this to you? Why is that?

DAVID: Because I don't get it. You're nervous and upset—so this is the place—

ANDREW: No, this isn't the time—

DAVID: Seems like the perfect time to me.

ANDREW: It's not.

DAVID: I don't like you here. I want to leave.

ANDREW: Just because I won't—

DAVID: You're embarrassed to be seen with me.

ANDREW: I'm not. I tell you I'm not—

DAVID: You jerked away from me.

ANDREW: I did not jerk. I moved. Like this. Watch me. That's what I did. Like this, see? This is what I did. That is not jerking.

DAVID: It was a jerk. That's either embarrassment or repulsion or fear.

ANDREW: I'm not doing this—

DAVID: And everytime I've tried to—

ANDREW: I'm not. And that's it.

DAVID: Okay. What do I know, Andrew, about what happened to you here?

ANDREW: That's right.

DAVID: I'm just a nice Jewish boy from Skokie.

ANDREW: Sometimes, you're nice. Sometimes, you're not so nice—

DAVID: *(Overlapping)* Okay, okay... And I know my parents indulged me so much that when kids started picking on me, they sent me to a different school— no expense spared.

ANDREW: Lucky you.

DAVID: Lucky me.

ANDREW: Exactly. And so what do you know, huh? What do you know?

DAVID: Nothing.

ANDREW: That's for sure.

DAVID: So tell me.

ANDREW: You don't know anything.

DAVID: Okay. I don't know anything.

ANDREW: That's for sure!!

DAVID: I love you and want to give you a little sense of comfort in a place that makes you feel so bad about yourself, but you won't let me do it. And I'm telling you now, I'm telling you now that what I want for myself—easy or not—is to get away from this damaged soul stuff—I want to get away from it—and what I want from a partner, a lover is that same thing. To get away. To get away from it.

ANDREW: Because I won't hold your hand, I'm damaged?

DAVID: Because you won't include me—

ANDREW: Won't include you? I'm damaged?

DAVID: Can I be a little bit more than the person who claims your body when you die?

ANDREW: What does that mean?

DAVID: Can I get close enough, can I be important enough to take your hand here in the lobby of your hometown nursing home without you being too scared to admit your feelings to me—

ANDREW: I do—

DAVID: —or to yourself or to the old man dribbling in his chair or to some hometown ghost—

ANDREW: I do.

DAVID: You don't.

ANDREW: I do!

DAVID: Because I won't stay—

ANDREW: *(Softly)* I do. I do.

DAVID: I will hold my lover's hand anywhere, Andrew, anywhere in the world—and no one, no one tells me that I don't have the right, that it's bad taste, that it makes someone uncomfortable. And I won't stay with anyone too frightened to do the same. But that is going to be so hard for me, because I thought, I'd been thinking that here he is, this is who I want. Andrew Morris. Age: Thirty-seven. Tall. Fair. In all things. Finally. You. And so it breaks my heart. It breaks my heart. To think about it. It does. It does.

(The lights crossfade to MAE *and* JAN. MAE *is standing with her crutches outside of her room. Her back is to the audience.* JAN *comes up to her.)*

JAN: Still having your temper tantrum? *(Beat)* Hello?
(Beat) Are you going in? *(Beat)* You want me to help
you? *(Beat)* You can't stay out here all day. *(Beat)*
The doctor says a week or so and then you can go
home. A week, that's all. That's not very long. But you
have to get up and move around more. You have to
keep moving. *(Beat. Then* JAN *touches* MAE*)* Come on.
Lets go in.

*(*MAE *withdraws slightly.)*

JAN: All right. *(Beat)* Do I need to get someone? *(Beat)*
If you won't come in, then I'll have to get someone.

MAE: You're moving when?

JAN: At the end of the semester.

MAE: End of the semester?

JAN: Twenty-four schools days from now.

MAE: Where?

JAN: To Bloomington.

MAE: You're going to live with Sarah?

JAN: No. Sarah has a boyfriend.

MAE: She lives with him?

JAN: Yes.

MAE: Oh...she must like him.

JAN: I think she does. Is that what this is about?

MAE: No. Have you found a place?

JAN: Not yet, but I'm going down this weekend,
and Sarah and I are going to look.

MAE: You could live with me.

JAN: I cannot live with you.

MAE: And why not?

JAN: Because I don't want to.

MAE: I could be at home. That's something to think about. If you were home, I could be, too.

JAN: I'm not taking care of you the rest of your life.

MAE: But if you were home—

JAN: I'm not taking care of you the rest of your life.

MAE: I wouldn't mind moving to Bloomington. I could get used to a bigger town.

JAN: No. Absolutely not.

MAE: Why?

JAN: Because, Mother, this phase of my life is over.

MAE: This phase? This phase?

JAN: Yes.

MAE: What do you mean, this phase?

JAN: This part of my life—

MAE: You know he visits everyday.

JAN: Who visits?

MAE: Chuck.

JAN: He visits you?

MAE: Everyday. Before I fell. After I fell. Everyday since you left.

JAN: He comes here?

MAE: Yes, he comes here.

JAN: I didn't know the two of you were so close.

MAE: We're not so close.

JAN: So what does he want then?

MAE: He just wants to figure out life, that's all.

JAN: *(Chuckling)* And so he comes to you?

MAE: Yes. *(Chuckling herself)* That is funny, isn't it?

JAN: And so what has he figured out? What have you helped him figure out?

MAE: A few things.

JAN: Such as?

MAE: None of your business.

JAN: All right.

MAE: I just thought you should know that he comes here and he talks to me and that he has been talking to me for a while. I just thought you should know.

JAN: Well, keep up the good work. *(She starts to exit.)*

MAE: Where are you going?

JAN: Back into the room.

MAE: What am I supposed to do?

JAN: Stand out here. Or come back in.

MAE: I want a cigarette.

JAN: Then go to the lounge.

MAE: By myself?

JAN: I think you can do it.

MAE: I don't have my cigarettes.

JAN: I'll put them here in your pocket.

MAE: You should go with me. *(Beat)* I said you should go with me.

JAN: I'm going to grade papers in the room.
(She continues moving.)

MAE: Stupid bitch!! You stupid, mean bitch!

JAN: *(Stopping, in a harsh whisper)* Don't you call me that.

MAE: You are a bitch, you know that?

JAN: I've told you—

MAE: A fucking bitch. Or should I say non-fucking bitch—

JAN: What?

MAE: And don't use that school teacher stuff with me—

JAN: I've told you never to use that word. That is a vile, ugly word used against women—

MAE: I used it against you.

JAN: I don't know what kind of conversations you're having with Chuck—

MAE: I want you to go with me.

JAN: I'm not going with you. In fact, I'm going into your room, gather up my things and leave.

MAE: *(Throwing her cigarettes to the floor)* I want a cigarette.

JAN: *(As she picks them up and puts them in* MAE's *pocket)* Then go have one.

VOICE *(Over P A. During this,* MAE *grabs the sleeve of* JAN's *sweater.* JAN *wiggles out of sweater and leaves with* MAE *holding sweater.)* Good morning, residents. This is Brenda. Today is Monday, April 15. Our resident of the day—tada—is Mae Anne Pierce in room 214. Mae Anne was born December 20, 1932—

MAE: *(Overlapping)* She said my age! You old bag! Fat bitch!

BRENDA: *(Overlapping)* And is a life long resident of Dixon. She was married twice—

MAE: *(Overlapping)* Oh, why does she have to say that? She hates me.

BRENDA: — to the late Benjamin Morris and Jimmy Pierce. She's probably best known as Dixon's answer to Connie Frances—

MAE: *(Overlapping)* I was better than Connie Francis—

BRENDA: *(Overlapping)* But according to Mae Anne, her proudest moment was singing to former President Ronald Reagan at the 1984 opening of the Reagan Boyhood Home. According to Mae, she didn't "wash my hips, I mean my lips for a week". *(She chuckles.)* She's funny, isn't she? Just a great gal.

MAE: *(Overlapping)* Fuck off.

BRENDA: (JAN *returns to get sweater during this)* And to help us celebrate this bright, new spring April 15 day, our resident of the day will be singing a selection of songs during the day's morning recreation.

(We hear one person applauding.)

BRENDA: So warm up those vocal cords. And we'll see you real soon!

(Beat. MAE *hands sweater to* JAN. *As* JAN *reaches for it,* MAE *drops it to the floor.* JAN *picks it up.)*

JAN: There you go, Mother. *(She leaves.)*

MAE: *(After looking around a bit)* All right, then.

(MAE *begins to move down the hallway as the lights crossfade to* DAVID. ANDREW *and* DAVID *look at one another. Then)*

ANDREW: Sounds like we're just in time. *(Beat)* I'm not sure what to say. Probably because I'm damaged.

DAVID: I don't mean for you to take it that way.

ANDREW: Oh, okay, then I'll take it another way.

DAVID: Can we—

ANDREW: And what does it mean? Damaged? What kind of bullshit is that? Damaged. Fucking damaged—

DAVID: Andrew—

ANDREW: You think that's going to make me open up to you—

DAVID: So you admit—

ANDREW: *(Continuing)* Saying bullshit like that—

DAVID: I told myself—

ANDREW: Who cares? You think I can't do this alone?

DAVID: I know you can.

ANDREW: You think I haven't been doing it by myself for the last thousand years?

DAVID: You're very self-sufficient.

ANDREW: That's right.

DAVID: Very controlled.

ANDREW: Yes... Very...all that. *(Beat)* I saw a ghost once.

DAVID: Really?

ANDREW: Yes. I did.

(Beat)

DAVID: Can I ask—

ANDREW: The sister who died? Alice Renee? A couple of weeks after, I was playing in the backyard—I was by myself—don't remember what I was doing exactly, but I do remember that I looked up at the house, and up at the second floor and, at the window of my parent's bedroom, as clear as day, was my sister, Alice. And she was looking down on me—right at me, I swear to God! And I remember that I said "Alice!" and then waved. A little wave. A shy, little wave because she didn't look happy and I wasn't sure if waving was the right thing to do. She did not wave back. And I never saw her again, but every time I was in the backyard, I'd look up to see if she was there. Her ghost—later— came in very handy. When I was in the second grade and kids started to pick on me—my parents did not send me to a special school—I would turn to them and say "You know, my sister died." And they'd back up. "Her name was Alice and she was ten." They'd back up a little more. "She died of leukemia." Back, back. "And now she looks at me from the upstairs window." Back, back, back. Staring at me, but quiet at last. Did I tell you this?

DAVID: No.

ANDREW: I didn't tell you? Funny. Good story, though, isn't it?

DAVID: *(Startled)* Yes.

ANDREW: Good story. Full of——oh, you know, all that great damaged soul stuff—

DAVID: Andy—

ANDREW: I had a big garden. Did I tell you that?

DAVID: No.

ANDREW: I did. I had a big garden. And my stepdad used to stand at the same window where I saw Alice and watch me working in my garden. I waved at him once, too, but..again, no response. He hated my flowers. Thought it was a weird thing for a teenage boy to be interested in. Sometimes he'd come outside and stand there watching me. Like he was John Wayne or something. "You quit that gardenin' or I'ma gonna kill ya." It was a beautiful garden, though, and I had the show ribbons to prove it. In fact, I used to wear the ribbons that I won around my neck—all around the place—sashay like this with my ribbons. Up in my bedroom, I'd imagine myself some kind of prince with all my ribbons to prove it. I never took the things off and Jimmy hated it. Hated it. And when I refused to take them off, he chased me out to the front lawn and around a tree—my mom flailing—her hands over her ears—the whole neighborhood watching, I'm sure—ribbons flying and my stepdad screaming "You sissy son of a bitch" —and my mom saying "Jimmy! Jimmy! Don't kill him! Don't kill him! We'll just have him move out!" And two days later, I was packing my bags and sitting on the front steps waiting for Ted and his mom to pick me up and carry me to a safe spot. I was sixteen the year my head fell. Like this I was all the time. *(He drops his head.)* Shame, shame, shame. This was me—I didn't mean for you to ever see this. Never, never, never were you supposed to see this. My head down so far I could practically carry it in my hands, like some ghostwalking decapitation.

(Beat. DAVID *lifts* ANDREW's *head.)*

ANDREW: *(As he drops his head)* Don't.

*(*DAVID *lifts it again.)*

ANDREW: *(Dropping his head again)* I said don't.

*(*DAVID *lifts it again and does some kind of adjustment that "keeps it in place". They look at one another.)*

DAVID: I get worried you know. There's always this arms length between us. *(Stretching out his arm)* About this far.

ANDREW: That far?

DAVID: It feels like it. I lie in bed beside you sometimes and I worry about it. That distance between us and I worry more because I don't think you know it's there and I don't know how to talk to you about it. ...That distance disappears for a brief few moments when you turn towards me in the morning—and you kiss me—and I think this is our purest time together. No memory of anything, really, except of us. But then the day and the memories somehow work themselves back. And you don't turn to me anymore. I don't know what happens, Andrew. And so the distance—

(ANDREW *suddenly tucks his head.* MAE *has limped on with her crutches. She walks past the both of them and looks out a window. Beat. As she looks,* ANDREW *curls his head further and further in to his lap.* MAE *does not notice them.* DAVID *watches* ANDREW *as he becomes increasingly more invisible.* MAE *walks past. She looks at them, smiles at* DAVID *and* ANDREW *who has looked up.* ANDREW *and* MAE *look at one another.* ANDREW *stands. He suddenly pulls* DAVID *up beside him. He takes David's hand and puts it up to his chest. A beat. She goes off. Beat)*

DAVID: That was her? ...Andy...that was her? Andy...Andy?

ANDREW: Goddamn her. Goddamn her.

(He stands there as the lights crossfade to CHUCK *on the phone.* TOMMY *sits there with* CHUCK, *pretending not to listen.)*

JAN: *(Answering phone in* MAE's *room)* Mae Pierce's room.

CHUCK: Jan. Chuck.

JAN: Hi, Chuck. *(Beat)* What is it, Chuck?

CHUCK: Smiley's sick.

JAN: He is?

CHUCK: I was wondering what I should do?

JAN: Take him to the vet.

CHUCK: I suppose I could do that.

(Beat)

JAN: What's wrong?

CHUCK: What if they think it's time?

JAN: Time for what?

CHUCK: To put him to sleep.

JAN: Then you'll just have to do it.

CHUCK: Oh.

JAN: He's seventeen.

CHUCK: I know.

JAN: It's a miracle he's lasted that long.

CHUCK: I suppose.

JAN: Do you want me to do it?

CHUCK: Take him in?

JAN: Yes.

CHUCK: No. I'll take him in. I'll see. I'll give him a couple of days. Should I call Sarah?

JAN: If you want. I'm not sure she cares that much anymore, but you might want to let her know all the same.

CHUCK: All right... How's your mom?

JAN: Okay.

CHUCK: Still depressed?

JAN: I suppose so.

CHUCK: Tell her I'll stop in.

JAN: Okay.

CHUCK: Has she told you I've been coming in?

JAN: She told me.

CHUCK: Well, I have been. I figured I should... Tommy's been here all morning—

JAN: You're with Fatboy?

CHUCK: He doesn't like to be called that anymore.

JAN: I can't help myself.

CHUCK: Well, he doesn't like it.

JAN: All right... Is there something else?

CHUCK: I'll see you tonight?

TOMMY: Now's a good time to ask.

JAN: *(Overlapping)* Yes. You know what you want for supper?

CHUCK: I hadn't thought about it.

JAN: Pork chops, maybe? There's some in the freezer if you can remember to take them out.

CHUCK: I'll take them out. One for you?

JAN: Do I ever stay for supper, Chuck?

CHUCK: No...

TOMMY: Now would be a good time to ask.

JAN: Is there something else?

CHUCK: Well, I've got another question for you.

JAN: And what is that?

CHUCK: Do you love me?

JAN: What?

CHUCK: Do you love me?

JAN: Why are you asking me that?

CHUCK: I want to know.

JAN: Did Fatboy put you up to this?

CHUCK: No, he did not. And stop calling him that!!

TOMMY: What?

JAN: I'm not having this conversation over the phone.

CHUCK: I'm sorry. I didn't mean to yell at you. I'm sorry. I think you should let me know.

JAN: Goodbye, Chuck.

CHUCK: Do you still love me?

JAN: I refuse to do this.

CHUCK: Please. *(Beat)* Answer the question. Please.

JAN: No, I don't.

CHUCK: What?

JAN: No.

CHUCK: What?

JAN: No, I said no. I don't love you.

(Beat)

CHUCK: Did you though? At one time? Did you? *(Beat)* Did you?

JAN: ...Yes.

CHUCK: Oh. But you stopped, right?

JAN: I stopped.

CHUCK: Okay. That's what I wanted to know. I needed to know that. I needed the information. *(Beat. Then suddenly)* You know, you told me you were going to clean out the basement!

JAN: And I will·

CHUCK: Goddamn it, you told me you were going to do it a long time ago. None of that stuff is mine! Not one goddamn thing down there is mine!

JAN: Plenty of it—

CHUCK: Not one goddamn thing!

TOMMY: Jesus, Chuck.

JAN: So I'll do it.

CHUCK: Well, I hope so! And there's other things! Other things! Why do I always have to get on you? Why is that, huh? And Fatboy will be here when you get here—he's not going home just because you're coming!

(Beat. TOMMY *is horrified.)*

CHUCK: *(Suddenly very soft)* So...I'll see you around six.... Around six or so? Jan? ...Hello?

*(*JAN, *quietly, hangs up. Lights fade on* JAN.*)*

TOMMY: What the hell were you doing? Chuck? What the hell was that? Are you crazy?

*(*CHUCK, *hiding his face, begins to cry.)*

TOMMY: What happened?

*(*CHUCK *continues to cry.)*

TOMMY: Oh boy. Oh boy. Catch your breath now. Catch your breath. Oh, boy. Oh boy, oh boy, oh boy. Hold on. Hold on. *(Rubbing* CHUCK's *back a little)* Things don't work out sometimes, do they?...I buy my wife a special gift for Christmas, a very special ring with a diamond. And when I go to hand it to her, she won't take it. The Jehovah's Witness don't believe in Christmas. And so I just stand there with my hand out, with this special gift, this special ring with a small diamond, the smallest diamond in the world, but at least my hands out. "I can't take that", she says. But I want you to have it, I say. My hand is reaching out like this—and she fixes me with that Jehovah's Witness look and says, "I don't want it." But I want you to have it— "No, no, no I don't want it." My hand's out the whole time. I'm embarrassed, ready to die, not sure how to bring my hand down. But I do. And instead of screaming like you did with Jan, I just go into the bathroom, say a few swear words like Goddamn fucking bitch and just cry

and cry and cry. But you know what I do with that
ring? I swallow it. Pulling myself up. Pulling myself
together, I swallow the smallest diamond ring in the
world. Down the hatch like a fucking aspirin! Poof!
Headaches gone! Poof! The veins relax, the brain opens
like a medical miracle. And that's what you've got to
do, Chuck. You've got to pull yourself up. Pull up and
pull out. Can you hear me? Are you listening? Up, up
now. Up, up, buddy. Up.

(The lights crossfade to JAN *who dials and then...)*

JAN: *(On the phone and in a bright voice)* Sarah, it's your
mom. I thought you might be— *(She begins to cry and
hangs up very quickly. Beat as she pulls herself together. She
dials again.)* Sarah, it's your mom again. I apologize for
hanging up...I thought you and Mike might be in class,
but on the off chance you weren't— *(She begins to cry
again.)* I have to— *(She hangs up. Beat. She gets herself
together and calls.)* Despite what you may think, your
poor mother is not losing her mind. Your grandmother
and your father are driving me crazy, that's true,
but otherwise, I'm all right. I wanted to tell you that I
will be down this weekend. I'm looking forward to it.
You have a list of places we can look at? I don't need
air-conditioning and I don't need a complex with a
pool. I was thinking an old house—an apartment onthe
second floor with a window looking out on the street. I
want to look out on the street through a shade tree. And
I will do what you suggest: Face forward and into the
wind! Bye, sweety. And hello to Mike—and apologies
for those ridiculous hang ups...ridiculous, ridiculous.

*(*MAE *has come in. She stands there as* JAN *hangs up.)*

MAE: You're here? Just can't get enough of this old bird,
can you? *(Beat)* I'm sorry. *(Beat)* I'm sorry. *(Beat)* I'm
sorry.

JAN: I can hear you, Mother.

MAE: Oh. Still no Andrew?

JAN: No. Did you have a cigarette?

MAE: Yes. He's not coming. I don't think he's coming.

JAN: Maybe there was traffic.

MAE: Did he say he was coming?

JAN: He said he was coming.

MAE: I don't think he is.

JAN: He said he was coming.

MAE: I don't think he'll make it. We might just as well forget it. Close the door and forget it. Can you can help me into bed?

JAN: Try it by yourself.

MAE: I cannot do it by myself.

JAN: Try it.

MAE: Boy, you never give up, do you? *(She struggles into the bed, groaning all the way.)*

JAN: I'd say you're about ready to go home.

MAE: I'm never leaving here. *(Beat)* You would think after all these years, he'd forget about it, wouldn't you?

JAN: I don't know, I'm not him.

MAE: Was I that bad?

JAN: You're concerned?

MAE: Was I?

JAN: You abandoned him.

MAE: I did not.

JAN: You did.

MAE: I protected him.

(JAN looks at her.)

MAE: Jimmy would have eventually killed him. I'm sure of that. *(Beat)* He wanted to live with those people. And I thought it was the best thing. *(Loudly)* I thought it was the best thing! *(Beat)* You make me so goddamn mad. He wanted to go! I said he wanted to go!

(JAN *still looks.)*

MAE: I protected him!!!!

JAN: You let Jimmy harass and threaten him—

MAE: Andrew flaunted himself—

JAN: He was in high school. He was sixteen.

MAE: I stood in between—

JAN: If I had been home—

MAE: You would have what?

JAN: I would have stopped him.

MAE: But you weren't, were you? You weren't home, were you?

JAN: No.

MAE: Were you, Miss Thing? Miss Teacher Thing.

JAN: No.

MAE: Where were you? ...Allrighty.

(Beat. JAN looks away.)

MAE: I think he liked living at Ted's, anyway. He said he did. And it was Jimmy's money that sent him to college. Sent him to Boston U. That was a very expensive school. *(Beat)* He has no business staying away this long. *(Beat)* He sends me money.

JAN: Does he?

MAE: Did you know that?

JAN: No.

MAE: He does. He sends me two hundred dollars a month.

JAN: I didn't know that.

MAE: He doesn't visit, but he sends money. And always with the same note. "Thought you might need this. Andrew." That's something, I guess. Isn't it?

JAN: That's something.

MAE: And I write him each time. A very short note, to thank him for the money—and each time I send him some kind of newspaper article or magazine article about something...about gay this or gay that, something I thought he might want to read or know about if he didn't already. "Thought you might want to see this," I say. Each time. "Thought you might want to see this." *(chuckling)* It took me forever to come up with that. "Thought you might want to see this." Forever that took. That was something, wasn't it?

JAN: I suppose it was.

MAE: ...You're pretty like my mom, you know it?

JAN: Mmmm.

MAE: You have her hair and profile. I always thought she was the prettiest mother in town. I thought about her when I fell and was lying on the ice and my whole life was passing in front of my eyes. And everything that had ever happened to me was racing around me and I kept thinking 'Hurry up. I can't stand seeing all this shit again!' It ended with the face of my mother smiling at me. I think she was welcoming me into the afterlife like a sweet mother angel. I'd thought she'd still be mad at me, but she wasn't. And I thought to myself "Just go numb. Let yourself melt into the ice and fly down into your mother's arms." *(She begins to cry.)* I had a dream last night. A terrible dream that woke me up.

JAN: What?

MAE: I dreamt that I was at home and you were a young girl and that I was chasing you around the house and beating you. You were asking me to stop, but I wouldn't. Somebody had to pull me off of you, but I can't remember who—

JAN: Mom—

MAE: *(Continuing)* Why would I have such a dream? After all, you're the one who took care of things. You did everything you were supposed to do.

JAN: I don't know.

MAE: Took care of me. Cleaned my house once a week! Took care of Alice, sweet thing that she was—

JAN: Don't talk about Alice.

MAE: Sweet thing that she was.

JAN: I said don't talk about her.

MAE: It hurts still, doesn't it? Thirty years later. And all that you did. Carried her from room to room. Her dried up little body, skinny as a bone—

JAN: I don't want you—

MAE: With her crying and screaming. Little bitty Andrew running behind you. Your dad in the basement rearranging the tools. Rearranging the tools. Sweeping the floor. But you were right there. And I thank you, Jan-thank you for what you did. Someone should have thanked you. I should have thanked you. Thank you for all you've done. We should have a thank you day for Jan. We should put up streamers. That's what we should do. How would you like it if we did something like that?

JAN: I wouldn't.

MAE: Come here, sweety.

JAN: I'm grading papers.

MAE: Come over here to me.

JAN: What do you need?

MAE: Just come over here.

JAN: No.

MAE: I'll give you a cherry chocolate.

(JAN *comes over.)*

MAE: I can't get this pillow, here. Can you reach over—

(JAN *does.* MAE *reaches up and pulls* JAN *into her.)*

JAN: What are you doing?

MAE: Let me give you a hug.

JAN: Don't do that. Let go of me.

MAE: Let me give my good daughter a big hug.

JAN: I don't want a hug. Let go of me. Mom!

(MAE *does.)*

JAN: How dare you do that?

MAE: Wha—?

JAN: How dare you try to hug me!!

MAE: I wha—?!

JAN: You never hugged me in your life. You've never even held my hand. And you want to hug me? You want to hug me, Mother? How dare you? *(She goes back to her grading.)*

BRENDA: *(Over the P A.)* Good morning, everyone. This is Brenda again. And today is Monday, April 15 and, ohhh, is it ever a wonderful, sunny, spring day. Take a look out your window! In just a few minutes, our resident of the day Mae Anne Pierce will be singing for us in the cafeteria. So get up! Take in the day! And sing-a-long with Mae Anne.

(MAE *gets her crutches. She walks over to* JAN *who does not look up.*)

MAE: I saw Andrew in the lobby. He's waiting in the lobby.

JAN: What?

MAE: Looking at me so hard—so angry—you tell him 'never mind'. Tell him that. Tell him "never mind".

(*She walks out of the room.* JAN *stands up and, in great frustration, holds both hands up and gives her the finger. The lights crossfade to lobby where* ANDREW *and* DAVID *sit.* ANDREW *still holds* DAVID'S *hand, but has his face half-buried in to his chest. We hear the last of* BRENDA'S *announcement.*)

BRENDA: (*Over P A*) The cafeteria is filling up so get yourself down here for the big Mae Anne Pierce sing-fest!!! This is going to be the big spring event here at Lee County!!!

DAVID: You okay? Andrew? Andy? I'm so sorry.... You breathing?

(ANDREW *nods.*)

DAVID: You weren't breathing for a while. I thought I was going to have to grab that guy's oxygen. But you're breathing, right?

(ANDREW *nods.*)

DAVID: Good.You're breaking my hand, by the way...no, no, no, no, no don't let go, just easier, just easier that's all...that's better...I like it. (*Beat*) *Why don't you come up? Come on up. She's gone. I think you scared the shit out of her. Scared the shit out of me, that's for sure. You were so fucking butch, whooaa, fucking butch, baby. Like a*

Ronald Reagan cowboy or something. Like Nancy Reagan on a horse.

ANDREW: *(Whispering)* I gotta get out of here.

DAVID: What?

ANDREW: I gotta get out of here.

DAVID: Okay.

ANDREW: Help me out of here.

DAVID: Sure.

ANDREW: I shouldn't have come—

DAVID: Maybe—

ANDREW: I don't think I should have.

DAVID: I'm sorry.

ANDREW: It's not your fault.

DAVID: It is.

ANDREW: No. It's not. I want to kill her before I leave. What if I kill her before we leave?

DAVID: We'll do it together.

ANDREW: *(Laughing a little)* Yes. We'll do it together.

DAVID: I'll push her out a window.

ANDREW: *(Looking at DAVID)* Hmph...I'm going to try, you know, David.

DAVID: I know.

ANDREW: Do you?

DAVID: Yes.

ANDREW: *(He stands.)* Okay, then.

(DAVID stands. A beat. DAVID takes ANDREW's hand.)

DAVID: Would you have anyone deny us this pleasure, Andrew?

(They exit. The lights crossfade to CHUCK *and* TOMMY. CHUCK *wipes his eyes.)*

TOMMY: You okay?

CHUCK: Okay.

TOMMY: You sure?

CHUCK: I'll be all right. *(He stares out.)* I used to think while I was lying in bed with Jan, I used to think about who was going to die first. I used to lay there and think—with Jan right there next to me—who was going to die first, me or Jan? I couldn't get to sleep thinking about it. I hoped that it would be me because I couldn't imagine what it would be like without her—

TOMMY: *(Quietly)* Pull up—

CHUCK: It's what I'm thinking—

TOMMY: It bothers me—

CHUCK: I can't help it—

TOMMY: You can pull up—

CHUCK: I can't be alone.

TOMMY: You're not alone. I'm here. And you've got Smiley there. He's hanging on. And, shit, I can cook. You got two pork chops in there, I'll cook it up. I'll eat with you.

CHUCK: You will?

TOMMY: I've got a wife who thinks I'm satan. So I'll cook. I don't mind.

CHUCK: You don't mind?

TOMMY: Why would I?

CHUCK: I don't know.

TOMMY: I'll tell you what. We take Smiley into the vet, get him all checked out, come on back home here and cook up some pork chops. How's it sound?

CHUCK: *(Quietly)* We take him in?

TOMMY: Sure.

CHUCK: Okay. *(He picks up the box and looks in. Quietly)* Smiley, old thing. Old pal. Old thing. I love ya. Love ya... Okay. Lets go.

(The lights crossfade to MAE's *room.* NORMA *comes in the room. She stops when she sees* JAN.)

JAN: Oh. Can I help you?

(The woman doesn't move.)

JAN: Can I help you?

(The woman takes out a folded newspaper article and hands it to JAN.)

JAN: What is this? *(She unfolds it and begins to read.)* "Nursing Home Resident Dated Hometown President". You dated President Reagan? Is this you? Norma Brown? The newspaper wrote an article about you, huh? That is very nice, very nice.

(The woman just stands there looking at JAN. JAN *reads the article.)*

JAN: This is you at the high school prom, isn't it? I think that's great. And you are both so handsome there. Tell me now, did he kiss you goodnight?

(Beat. NORMA *stares at her.)*

JAN: I'll bet he did, didn't he? I'll bet.

(Beat. She gives the article back to NORMA *who stands there.)*

JAN: Would you like a cherry chocolate?

*(*JAN *offers her the cherry chocolates. The woman takes one.)*

JAN: You can have more. Go ahead. Take all that you want.

(Beat. NORMA takes one. JAN keeps the box in front of her. NORMA continues to take one and then another and another. JAN starts to laugh as the woman takes them. NORMA begins to smile with her. When she has finished, there is a beat.)

JAN: How about some cigarettes? Would you like some cigarettes?

(JAN begins to give NORMA all of MAE's cigarettes, stuffing them into NORMA's pockets. NORMA laughs as she does so.)

JAN: *(Laughing with NORMA)* That's right! You laugh! You laugh! In here. And here. And there.

(NORMA looks at JAN. She smiles at her.)

JAN: Anything else I can get you?

(NORMA looks at JAN smiling. She suddenly hugs JAN very tightly. JAN tenses at first, but then slowly hugs her back.)

JAN: Now...you need to let go of me, honey.... You need to let go.... Come on now... Come on...what a big hug... Come on... Such a big, big hug... Well...well... A little hug back... Hmmm... You lost all your memory, but you kept this, didn't you? This you didn't forget.... I have a daughter named Sarah. She's twenty-two. And a graduate student. And soon I'll be living very near her....I have a daughter named Sarah. She's twenty two. And soon I'll be living near her. *(Still hugging NORMA)* I have a daughter named Sarah. Yes. And I'll be living near her very soon. Remember that. Yes. Very soon. Very soon.

(The lights crossfade to MAE sitting in a chair—center stage. MAE is in her element. She has a microphone in her hand.)

MAE: Hello, everyone— *(Looking out)* —Oh my God, look at you people, you're all in wheelchairs! I feel like I'm in old folks home! *(She cackles loudly.)* And what

happened to you, honey? Stroke? Did you have a
stroke? Yes? I'm so sorry. Is that what's wrong with
your hand? But you're hanging in there, aren't you,
honey? How about a little applause for this beautiful
woman here.

(One person applauds.)

MAE: I take one look at you and say "there but for
the grace of God, go I. Go me. Whatever." *(She cackles
loudly.)* Is it hot in here? You say you're hot, honey? I'd
say you haven't been hot since 1952. *(She cackles loudly.)*
Have I told you my *Puss and Boots* story? Oh, I love the
puss and the boot story because it's such a dirty, dirty
story that's all about a great big, black boot and two
sweet pu—oh my God, Seizure!! Over there!! Seizure!!!
(She cackles.) You are such a fun crowd, you know that?
Give yourself a hand.

(One person applauds.)

MAE: So I guess I'm here to sing a couple of songs for
you.

(One person applauds.)

MAE: Thank you sir. Give that guy a better seat!
(She cackles.) Now I thought I would start with one
of my favorites, and I hope it's one of your's, too.
It's called "I Walk the Line" and boy, have I ever.
Life's hard, you know? You walk the line, you walk
life and that's all there is to it. Ronald Reagan walked
that line and helped me walk it, too.

(One person applauds.)

MAE: You out there, Ronny? Can you hear me? This is
for you, you sweet, sweet, sweet goodlooking thing.

(One person applauds.)

MAE: And a one and a two and a three—

(A piano begins to play I Walk the Line.*)*

MAE: Faster, honey. Faster.

(The music begins to play. MAE *begins to sing with the recording as of the Johnny Cash version of* I Walk the Lines. *As* MAE *sings in background.* JAN *walks into lobby as* ANDREW *and* DAVID *are walking out. They look at one another. Beat.* JAN, *tentatively, waves at* ANDREW. *He returns the wave as the lights cross fade and* MAE *finishes her singing.)*

(Curtain)

END OF PLAY